THE REAL
Violet Jessop

45th Parallel Press

Published in the United States of America by Cherry Lake Publishing
Ann Arbor, Michigan
www.cherrylakepublishing.com

Reading Adviser: Marla Conn MS, Ed., Literacy specialist, Read-Ability, Inc.
Book Cover Design: Felicia Macheske

Photo Credits: © Dmitry Laudin/Shutterstock.com, Cover, 1; © CK Foto/Shutterstock.com, Cover, 1; © antoniradso/Shutterstock.com, 5; © Everett Historical/Shutterstock.com, 7, 20; © andipantz/iStock, 9; © Anneka/Shutterstock.com, 11; © ilbusca/iStock, 12; © Library of Congress/Reproduction No. LC-DIG-ggbain-10339, 15; © Yuangeng Zhang / Shutterstock.com,17; © Library of Congress/Johnston, J.S. [1890-1903]/Reproduction No. LC-DIG-det-4a15884, 23; © duncan1890/iStock, 24; © Allen.G/ Shutterstock.com, 27; © Library of Congress/Reproduction No. LC-DIG-npcc-03846, 29; Public Domain/ United Kingdom Government, 30

Graphic Elements Throughout: © iulias/Shutterstock.com; © Thinglass/Shutterstock.com; © kzww/ Shutterstock.com; © A_Lesik/Shutterstock.com; © MegaShabanov/Shutterstock.com; © Groundback Atelier/Shutterstock.com; © saki80/Shutterstock.com

45th Parallel Press is an imprint of Cherry Lake Publishing.

Library of Congress Cataloging-in-Publication Data

Names: Loh-Hagan, Virginia, author.
Title: The real Violet Jessop / by Virginia Loh-Hagan.
Description: Ann Arbor, Michigan : Cherry Lake Publishing, [2019] | Series: History Uncut |
    Includes bibliographical references and index.
Identifiers: LCCN 2018035191 | ISBN 9781534143364 (hardcover) | ISBN 9781534141124 (pdf) |
    ISBN 9781534139923 (pbk.) | ISBN 9781534142329 (hosted ebook)
Subjects: LCSH: Jessop, Violet, 1887-1971,—Juvenile literature. |
    Shipwreck survival—North Altantic Ocean—Juvenile literature. | Titanic (Steamship)—Juvenile literature. |
    Britannic (Ship)—Juvenile literature. | Shipwrecks—North Atlantic Ocean—Juvenile literature. |
    Shipwrecks—Aegean Sea—Juvenile literature.
Classification: LCC G530.J45 L64 2019 | DDC 910.9163/4—dc23
LC record available at https://lccn.loc.gov/2018035191

Cherry Lake Publishing would like to acknowledge the work of The Partnership for 21st Century Skills. Please visit www.p21.org for more information.

Printed in the United States of America
Corporate Graphics

Table of Contents

CHAPTER 1

Violet Jessop
The Story You Know

Everyone knows about the sinking of the *Titanic*. The *Titanic* was a ship. It was supposed to be unsinkable. Unsinkable means not having the ability to sink. But then it hit an iceberg. Icebergs are big floating chunks of ice. The *Titanic* sank. There were only about 700 survivors. Survivors are people who live through something bad.

One of the survivors was Violet Constance Jessop. But she was a special survivor. She lived through three disasters at sea. Unlike the *Titanic*, Jessop was unsinkable.

Jessop's life is inspiring. But there's more to her story ...

There were about 2,200 people on board the *Titanic*.

CHAPTER 2

Survivor from the Start

Jessop's parents were William and Katherine. William was a sheep farmer. Katherine's family had a photography business. William and Katherine were married in 1886.

They were Irish **immigrants**. Immigrants are people who move from another country. Things weren't good in Ireland. People were hungry. They didn't have jobs. They weren't treated fairly. Many Irish people moved to the Americas. That's how they survived.

William moved the family to Argentina. He got a job as a manager of a railroad station. Jessop was born on October 2, 1887. She was born in the **Pampas**. Pampas are plains. They're flat lands without trees.

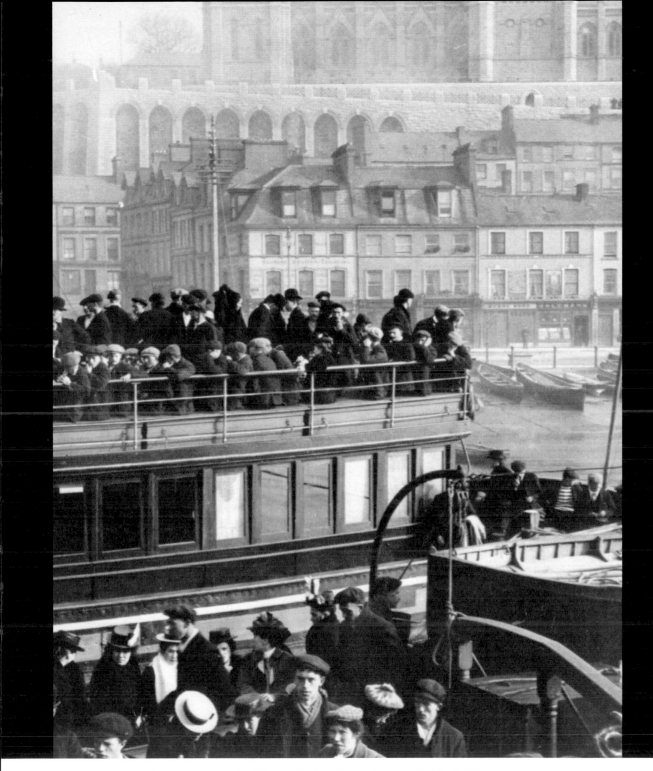

Between 1845 and 1850, about 500,000 Irish
people moved to the United States.

SETTING THE WORLD STAGE

1887

> The U.S. Senate let the U.S. Navy lease Pearl Harbor. Lease means to rent. The navy wanted to use Pearl Harbor as a naval base. Pearl Harbor is on the island of Oahu, Hawaii. It houses the main offices of the U.S. Pacific Fleet.

> Construction started on the Eiffel Tower. The Eiffel Tower is in Paris, France. It was built for the 1889 World's Fair. But today, it has become the symbol of France. It's famous. It's the most visited monument in the world. It's 1,063 feet (324 meters) tall.

> The 1887 Yellow River Flood began in China. It was caused by heavy rainfall overflowing the river's banks. It killed over 900,000 people. Over 2 million others lost their homes.

> Arthur Conan Doyle created Sherlock Holmes. Holmes made his first appearance in 1887. He was in a book called *A Study in Scarlet.* Scarlet means red.

"Surely, it is all a dream." — Violet Jessop

Jessop was the oldest of 9 children. Only 6 of the children survived. Three children died as babies. Not many children lived to be adults at this time. Cities were crowded. Food and water were dirty. Not many people could pay for doctors.

Jessop was the oldest daughter. So, she took care of her brothers and sisters. But she also got sick. She may have had **tuberculosis**. This can be a deadly sickness. It's when bad germs attack the lungs. Doctors didn't think Jessop would survive. They gave her only months to live. But Jessop surprised them. She lived through it.

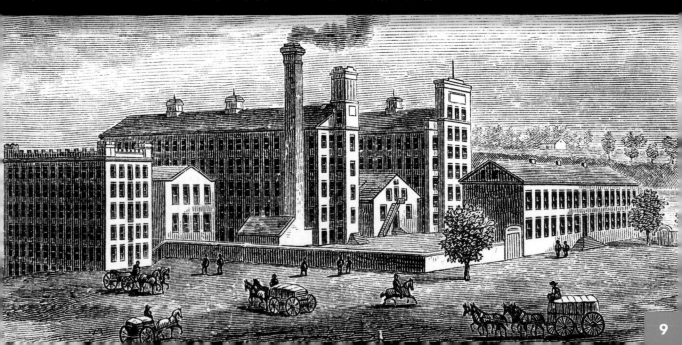

Jessop lived during the Industrial Revolution.
Cities and factories were taking over.

CHAPTER 3

Like Mother, Like Daughter

At age 16, Jessop's father died. He got **cancer**. Cancer is a sickness. It's hard to cure.

Jessop's mother moved the family to England. Jessop went to a **convent school**. Convent schools are for girls. They're run by nuns.

The family needed money. Jessop's mother got a job working on ships. She was a **stewardess**. A stewardess is a female **steward**. Stewards serve people on ships. They clean **cabins**. Cabins are rooms on ships.

Jessop cared for the children when her mother was out to sea. Then, her mother got sick. Jessop left school. She needed to work.

Convent schools are religious.

She applied to be a stewardess. But she had a hard time. No one would hire her. Most of the women working on ships were older. They looked plain. The bosses didn't want women to distract others. Jessop was young. She was pretty. She had to dress down. She wore old clothes. She couldn't wear makeup.

At age 21, she was hired by the Royal Mail Line. She worked hard. She worked 17 hours a day. Two years later, she was hired by the White Star Line. She wasn't happy about this. She didn't want to sail the North Atlantic Ocean. She knew the weather was bad. She also heard stories about the demanding **passengers**. Passengers are people who travel on ships.

The first ship Jessop worked on was the *Orinoco*.

All in the Family

There's another person who's called "unsinkable." Maggie Brown is called "The Unsinkable Mrs. Brown." Both Brown and Jessop survived the *Titanic* disaster. Brown helped people when the ship started sinking. She got people on the lifeboats. She was on lifeboat number 6. She helped paddle. She kept people's spirits up. She urged the crew to return to get survivors. She said she'd throw people overboard if they didn't help. She organized a survivors' committee. She became famous. She used her fame to help others. She lived from 1867 to 1932. She was an American. She was born poor. But she became very rich when her husband's mining company did well. She did a lot of community service. She helped start the first U.S. court for young people. She supported women's rights. She was one of the first women to run for office. She did this before women had the right to vote.

"My brain shook like a solid body in a bottle of liquid." – Violet Jessop

CHAPTER 4

First Crash

In 1910, Jessop worked on the *Olympic*. She worked for the White Star Line. Until 1912, the *Olympic* was the world's biggest ship. It was the first in a new class of **luxury** ships. Luxury means fancy.

On September 20, 1911, the ship left England. This was the ship's fifth trip. It tried to make a turn. It crashed into the *Hawke*. The *Hawke* was a British warship. It tore two big holes in the *Olympic*. This caused some **flooding**. Flooding is an overflow of water.

The people on the ship were dropped off at the nearest **port**. Ports are places where ships can dock or land.

The *Olympic* had a long service life. It was in use for 24 years.

THAT Happened?!?

The *Britannic* was a sister ship to the *Titanic*. It was launched 2 years after the *Titanic* sank. Like the *Titanic*, the *Britannic* also sank. For over 100 years, the *Britannic* has lived on the ocean floor. There was a meeting to discuss what to do with the ship's remains. There were scientists. There were divers. Yiannis Tsavelakos was there. He owns a diving company in Greece. He teaches people to dive. He gives people diving tours. He wants to do something with the wreck. He wants to turn it into an underwater theme park. Theme parks have rides and games. They're built for fun. The *Britannic* park would be designed for divers. Divers would be able to explore the wreck. Tsavelakos's dream is to build an underwater park. But many people don't want to touch it. The ship is a "war grave." Over 30 people lost their lives. They're buried in the ship.

"I hated the wind . . . It made me gloomy and sad . . . I loved the rain. And the smell of the earth after the rain was the loveliest perfume of all." – Violet Jessop

Nobody was hurt. Both ships were damaged. But they didn't sink. They made it back to port. They were fixed up. They were sent out to sea again.

It took about 2 months to fix the *Olympic*. The shipbuilders used parts from a new ship they were building. That new ship was called the *Titanic*. This delayed the completion of the *Titanic*.

This was Jessop's first crash at sea. Most people would get scared. But she didn't quit. Seven months later, she went back to work.

The White Star Line wanted the *Olympic* to be fixed as soon as possible. It wanted people to know their ships were strong.

CHAPTER 5

Iceberg Ahead!

Jessop was happy on the *Olympic*. But her friends kept telling her about the White Star Line's new ship. The *Titanic* was a sister ship to the *Olympic*. It was bigger. It was fancier. And it was supposed to be unsinkable. Jessop's friends told her it would be a "wonderful experience."

Jessop signed up. She was ready to work on the *Titanic*'s **maiden voyage**. Maiden voyage means the first trip. Jessop brought a special prayer. The prayer was supposed to protect her against fire and water.

On April 10, 1912, the *Titanic* hit an iceberg. It started to sink. In 2 hours, the ship was underwater.

The iceberg was thought to be about 50 to 100 feet (15.2 to 30.5 m) high and 200 to 400 feet (60.9 to 121.9 m) long!

Jessop was "comfortably **drowsy**" when the ship crashed. Drowsy means sleepy. Jessop was ordered on deck. She helped the confused passengers. She helped people get into lifeboats. She was ordered to get into lifeboat number 16. She showed people how safe it was. One of the sailors gave her a baby. He said, "Here, Miss Jessop. Look after this baby."

Jessop was on the freezing lifeboat for 8 hours. The next morning, Jessop was rescued by the *Carpathia*. On that ship, the mother grabbed the baby. She ran off. Jessop said, "I was too frozen and **numb** to think it strange that this woman had not stopped to say, 'Thank you.' " Numb means not being able to feel.

More than 1,500 lives were lost that night.

Bad Blood

At age 36, Jessop got married. Not much is known about him. But some people found their marriage papers. Her husband appears to be John James Lewis. Lewis was a fellow steward. He worked on several ships, including the *Olympic*. He met Jessop on the *Majestic* in 1923. The ship was completing its 10th trip to New York. Jessop and Lewis went back to London. They got married 4 days after landing. They got married in a church. They got married on a Monday. Not many people were at their wedding. Lewis was 10 years older than Jessop. His father was a ship's captain. Lewis was the oldest of three sons. He was from Liverpool. Jessop and Lewis weren't happy. They didn't get along. They divorced a year later. They didn't have any children. Lewis died in 1959. Some records show he may have also survived the *Titanic*.

"Life was much simpler then: A man was taken at his worth all the time." — Violet Jessop

CHAPTER 6

Third Time Is a Charm

Jessop kept working. In 1916, she worked on the *Britannic*. This ship was nicknamed "Titanic 2." It had more lifeboats. It was also supposed to be unsinkable.

During World War 1, the White Star Line turned some of its ships into hospital ships. The *Britannic* was one of them. Its job was to return hurt soldiers to England. Jessop worked with the American Red Cross. She became a nurse on the ship.

On November 21, 1916, the *Britannic* was in the Aegean Sea. It got hit. It may have been hit by a **torpedo**. Torpedoes are missiles. Or the ship was hit by a German **mine**. Mines are bombs that go off when sparked.

The *Britannic* had 1,125 people on board the ship.

Jessop was in the ship's kitchen when the ship got hit. She was holding a teapot. She got in a lifeboat. She watched the ship sink. The ship sank in 1 hour. It killed 30 people. It almost killed Jessop.

As the ship was sinking, the **propellers** were still spinning. Propellers are blades that help move ships. The spinning was sucking in the lifeboats. It was chopping up everything. Jessop jumped out of her lifeboat in time. But she hit her head. Another lifeboat saved her. Jessop escaped.

But years later, she got a lot of headaches. She went to her doctor. Her doctor told her she had broken her skull.

The *Britannic* survivors were rescued by the Royal Navy.

CHAPTER 7

Unsinkable

Jessop learned a lesson from her ship crashes. After the *Titanic*, Jessop had wanted her toothbrush. So, when the *Britannic* sank, she remembered her toothbrush. She grabbed it. Then, she jumped overboard.

Jessop didn't let her near-death experiences stop her. She still worked on ships. After the war, ship travel became popular. More people went on **cruises**. Cruises are vacations on ships. Jessop worked for cruise companies. She didn't have any more sea crashes.

She worked on ships for 42 years. She sailed around the world twice. She finally retired. She lived in England. She raised chickens. She worked on her gardens.

Jessop joined the Red Star Line.

Explained by
SCIENCE

Icebergs are big floating ice chunks. They're not sea ice. Sea ice is frozen seawater. It's made of saltwater. Icebergs are made of freshwater. They're part of glaciers. Glaciers are big slabs of ice and snow. They build over thousands of years. There are layers of ice. Icebergs break off of glaciers. This process is called calving. Icebergs fall into the ocean. They make big waves. They float around. They live for 3 to 6 years before melting away. If they move into warm water, they'll melt. They wash away over time when waves hit. They come in many shapes and sizes. Growlers are the smallest ones. They're about the size of cars. Bergy bits are the size of houses. The other sizes are small, medium, large, and very large. Icebergs can be over 240 feet (73 m) high. They can be 670 feet (204 m) long. They form near the North and South Poles.

"Gently, *Titanic* disengaged herself from the side of the dock and we were off on a soft April day." – Violet Jessop

She got a phone call. It was a stormy night. There was a woman on the phone. She asked if Jessop had saved a baby on the *Titanic*. Jessop said, "Yes." The woman said, "I was that baby." She laughed and then hung up. People told Jessop it was a **prank** call. Pranks are jokes. People thought kids in the village were calling. But Jessop didn't think it was a prank.

She died at age 83. She died of heart problems. She stayed afloat until the end.

Jessop never told anyone about the baby until after she got the call.

Timeline

1887: Jessop was born on October 2. She was born near Bahia Blanca, Argentina.

1908: Jessop was hired at the Royal Mail Line. This was the largest shipping company in the world. It ran tours. It delivered mail. It went from England to South America.

1910: Jessop was transferred to the White Star Line. This was a famous British shipping company. It sailed between Britain, Australia, and America. The *Olympic* was part of this shipping company.

1911: Jessop worked on the *Olympic* when it hit another ship. The *Olympic* was built right before the *Titanic*. It was about 3 inches (7.6 centimeters) smaller. It was not as heavy. This was the year the *Olympic* hit another ship.

1912: Jessop worked on the *Titanic*. This ship was the world's largest passenger ship. It burned 600 tons of coal a day. Over 170 men were needed to shovel in the coal.

1916: Jessop worked on the *Britannic*. Its original name was the *Gigantic*. After the *Titanic* sank, its design was changed. It was made safe from icebergs.

1923: Jessop got married 3 weeks after her birthday. She got divorced. Their marriage was short.

1935: The *Olympic* was nicknamed "Old Reliable." It was scrapped after 24 years of service. Scrapped means broken down into parts.

1950: Jessop moved to Suffolk in England. Suffolk is the farthest east one can go in the United Kingdom. It's the first place in the country to see the sunrise.

1971: Jessop died. She was 83 years old.

1975: Jacques Cousteau was an underwater explorer and scientist. He found the wreck of the *Britannic*. He found it 400 feet (122 m) below the sea.

1985: Robert Ballard is an underwater scientist. He found the wreck of the *Titanic*. He found it 12,415 feet (3,784 m) below the sea.

1998: Jessop's memoir was published. It is called *Titanic Survivor*.